O'

by Iain Gray

Lang**Syne**

PUBLISHING

WRITING *to* REMEMBER

LangSyne

PUBLISHING

WRITING *to* REMEMBER

Office 5, Vineyard Business Centre,
Pathhead, Midlothian EH37 5XP
Tel: 01875 321 203 Fax: 01875 321 233
E-mail: info@lang-syne.co.uk
www.langsyneshop.co.uk

Design by Dorothy Meikle
Printed by Hay Nisbet Press, Glasgow
© Lang Syne Publishers Ltd 2009

ISBN 978-1-85217-336-4

O'Shea

MOTTO:
To seek the truth.

CREST:
A black swan.

NAME variations include:
Ó Séaghdha (*Gaelic*)
Ó Shéaghdha (*Gaelic*)
O'Shee
McShea
McShee
Shea
Shee

Chapter one:
Origins of Irish surnames

**According to an old saying, there are two types of Irish –
those who actually are Irish and those who wish they were.**

This sentiment is only one example of the allure that the
high romance and drama of the proud nation's history holds
for thousands of people scattered across the world today.

It's a sad fact, however, that the vast majority of Irish
surnames are found far beyond Irish shores, rather than on
the Emerald Isle itself.

The population stood at around eight million souls in
1841, but today it stands at fewer than six million.

This is mainly a tragic consequence of the potato
famine, also known as the Great Hunger, which devastated
Ireland between 1845 and 1849.

The Irish peasantry had become almost wholly reliant
for basic sustenance on the potato, first introduced from the
Americas in the seventeenth century.

When the crop was hit by a blight, at least 800,000
people starved to death while an estimated two million
others were forced to seek a new life far from their native
shores – particularly in America, Canada, and Australia.

The effects of the potato blight continued until about
1851, by which time a firm pattern of emigration had
become established.

Ireland's loss, however, was to the gain of the countries in which the immigrants settled, contributing enormously, as their descendants do today, to the well being of the nations in which their forefathers settled.

But those who were forced through dire circumstance to establish a new life in foreign parts never forgot their roots, or the proud heritage and traditions of the land that gave them birth.

Nor do their descendants.

It is a heritage that is inextricably bound up in the colourful variety of Irish names themselves – and the origin and history of these names forms an integral part of the vibrant drama that is the nation's history, one of both glorious fortune and tragic misfortune.

This history is well documented, and one of the most important and fascinating of the earliest sources are *The Annals of the Four Masters*, compiled between 1632 and 1636 by four friars at the Franciscan Monastery in County Donegal.

Compiled from earlier sources, and purporting to go back to the Biblical Deluge, much of the material takes in the mythological origins and history of Ireland and the Irish.

This includes tales of successive waves of invaders and settlers such as the Fomorians, the Partholonians, the Nemedians, the Fir Bolgs, the Tuatha De Danann, and the Laigain.

Of particular interest are the *Milesian Genealogies*,

because the majority of Irish clans today claim a descent from either Heremon, Ir, or Heber – three of the sons of Milesius, a king of what is now modern day Spain.

These sons invaded Ireland in the second millennium B.C, apparently in fulfilment of a mysterious prophecy received by their father.

This Milesian lineage is said to have ruled Ireland for nearly 3,000 years, until the island came under the sway of England's King Henry II in 1171 following what is known as the Cambro-Norman invasion.

This is an important date not only in Irish history in general, but for the effect the invasion subsequently had for Irish surnames.

'Cambro' comes from the Welsh, and 'Cambro-Norman' describes those Welsh knights of Norman origin who invaded Ireland.

But they were invaders who stayed, inter-marrying with the native Irish population and founding their own proud dynasties that bore Cambro-Norman names such as Archer, Barbour, Brannagh, Fitzgerald, Fitzgibbon, Fleming, Joyce, Plunkett, and Walsh – to name only a few.

These 'Cambro-Norman' surnames that still flourish throughout the world today form one of the three main categories in which Irish names can be placed – those of Gaelic-Irish, Cambro-Norman, and Anglo-Irish.

Previous to the Cambro-Norman invasion of the twelfth century, and throughout the earlier invasions and settlement of those wild bands of sea rovers known as the Vikings in the eighth and ninth centuries, the population of the island was relatively small, and it was normal for a person to be identified through the use of only a forename.

But as population gradually increased and there were many more people with the same forename, surnames were adopted to distinguish one person, or one community, from another.

Individuals identified themselves with their own particular tribe, or 'tuath', and this tribe – that also became known as a clann, or clan – took its name from some distinguished ancestor who had founded the clan.

The Gaelic-Irish form of the name Kelly, for example, is Ó Ceallaigh, or O'Kelly, indicating descent from an original 'Ceallaigh', with the 'O' denoting 'grandson of.' The name was later anglicised to Kelly.

The prefix 'Mac' or 'Mc', meanwhile, as with the clans of the Scottish Highlands, denotes 'son of.'

Although the Irish clans had much in common with their Scottish counterparts, one important difference lies in what are known as 'septs', or branches, of the clan.

Septs of Scottish clans were groups who often bore an entirely different name from the clan name but were under the clan's protection.

In Ireland, septs were groups that shared the same name and who could be found scattered throughout the four provinces of Ulster, Leinster, Munster, and Connacht.

The 'golden age' of the Gaelic-Irish clans, infused as their veins were with the blood of Celts, pre-dates the Viking invasions of the eighth and ninth centuries and the Norman invasion of the twelfth century, and the sacred heart of the country was the Hill of Tara, near the River Boyne, in County Meath.

Known in Gaelic as 'Teamhar na Rí', or Hill of Kings, it was the royal seat of the 'Ard Rí Éireann', or High King of Ireland, to whom the petty kings, or chieftains, from the island's provinces were ultimately subordinate.

It was on the Hill of Tara, beside a stone pillar known as the Irish 'Lia Fáil', or Stone of Destiny, that the High Kings were inaugurated and, according to legend, this stone would emit a piercing screech that could be heard all over Ireland when touched by the hand of the rightful king.

The Hill of Tara is today one of the island's main tourist attractions.

Opposition to English rule over Ireland, established in the wake of the Cambro-Norman invasion, broke out frequently and the harsh solution adopted by the powerful forces of the Crown was to forcibly evict the native Irish from their lands.

These lands were then granted to Protestant colonists, or 'planters', from Britain.

Many of these colonists, ironically, came from Scotland and were the descendants of the original 'Scotti', or 'Scots', who gave their name to Scotland after migrating there in the fifth century A.D., from the north of Ireland.

Colonisation entailed harsh penal laws being imposed on the majority of the native Irish population, stripping them practically of all of their rights.

The Crown's main bastion in Ireland was Dublin and its environs, known as the Pale, and it was the dispossessed peasantry who lived outside this Pale, desperately striving to eke out a meagre living.

It was this that gave rise to the modern-day expression of someone or something being 'beyond the pale'.

Attempts were made to stamp out all aspects of the ancient Gaelic-Irish culture, to the extent that even to bear a Gaelic-Irish name was to invite discrimination.

This is why many Gaelic-Irish names were anglicised with, for example, and noted above, Ó Ceallaigh, or O'Kelly, being anglicised to Kelly.

Succeeding centuries have seen strong revivals of Gaelic-Irish consciousness, however, and this has led to many families reverting back to the original form of their name, while the language itself is frequently found on the fluent tongues of an estimated 90,000 to 145,000 of the island's population.

Ireland's turbulent history of religious and political strife is one that lasted well into the twentieth century, a landmark century that saw the partition of the island into the twenty-six counties of the independent Republic of

Ireland, or Eire, and the six counties of Northern Ireland, or Ulster.

Dublin, originally founded by Vikings, is now a vibrant and truly cosmopolitan city while the proud city of Belfast is one of the jewels in the crown of Ulster.

It was Saint Patrick who first brought the light of Christianity to Ireland in the fifth century A.D.

Interpretations of this Christian message have varied over the centuries, often leading to bitter sectarian conflict – but the many intricately sculpted Celtic Crosses found all over the island are symbolic of a unity that crosses the sectarian divide.

It is an image that fuses the 'old gods' of the Celts with Christianity.

All the signs from the early years of this new millennium indicate that sectarian strife may soon become a thing of the past – with the Irish and their many kinsfolk across the world, be they Protestant or Catholic, finding common purpose in the rich tapestry of their shared heritage.

Chapter two:

The Black Swan

One clue to the truly ancient roots of the proud clan of O'Shea lies in the fact that their Coat of Arms features a black swan.

The swan forms an integral part of Celtic mythology, considered as it was as representative of not only the power of healing and the gift of music but also of purity and love.

Thought by the Celts to encapsulate the primary elements of earth, wind and water, the swan was also regarded as being able to 'shape shift' – assuming the shape of humans whenever the fancy took them.

This has a thrilling resonance in the Celtic legend of the Children of Lir – who were miraculously transformed into swans. The *eala dubh*, or black swan, also features in the O'Shea battle cry of *Eala dubh Abú*, meaning 'The Black Swan Forever.'

The Gaelic Irish forms of the name are Ó Séaghdha and Ó Shéaghdha, stemming from 'Seaghdha', indicating 'hawklike' or, according to some authorities, 'stately.'

Present day Co. Kerry in Munster which, along with Ulster, Leinster and Connacht is one of Ireland's four ancient provinces, is the original territory of the O'Sheas, but they later became particularly associated with the county of Kilkenny.

Their ancestry is illustrious, descended as they are from one of Ireland's earliest monarchs.

This is Heremon, who along with Heber, Ir and Amergin, was a son of Milesius, a king of what is now modern day Spain, and who had planned to invade the island in fulfilment of a mysterious Druidic prophecy.

Milesius died before he could embark on the invasion, but his sons successfully undertook the daunting task in his stead in about 1699 B.C.

Legend holds that their invasion fleet was scattered in a storm and Ir killed when his ship was driven onto the island of Scellig-Mhicheal, off the coast of modern day Co. Kerry.

Only Heremon, Heber and Amergin survived, although Ir left issue.

Heremon and Heber became the first of the Milesian monarchs of Ireland, but Heremon later killed Heber in a quarrel said to have been caused by their wives, while Amergin was slain by Heremon in an argument over territory.

Along with the O'Sheas, other clans that trace a descent from Heremon include those of Cassidy, Donnelly, Higgins, Kelly, McKenna, McManus, Callaghan, O'Connor and Traynor.

Many distinguished Irish kings were of the noble line of Heremon.

They include Irial Fiada, one of his sons, and the 10th monarch of Ireland.

Recognised as very learned and with the gift of second sight, it was Irial, who died in 1670 B.C., who was responsible for clearing much of the island of its dense forests.

Also of the Heremonian line of kings was Tigernmas, the 13th monarch of Ireland.

Said to have worshipped a mysterious idol known as 'Crom Cruach', it was Tigernmas who introduced the wearing of colours as a means of distinguishing rank.

A soldier would wear three colours, while a king or queen would wear six – and some authorities assert this may be the origins of the plaid, or tartan, worn centuries later by those originally native Irish who had settled in the Highlands and Islands of Scotland.

The 66th monarch of the line of Heremon, Ugaine Mór, appears to have been particularly enterprising.

This king, who died in 593 B.C., is reputed to have landed with a Celtic army in Africa, while he later married a daughter of the king of the Gauls.

But arguably the most notable of the Heremonian line of Irish monarchs was Cormac Mac Art.

Recognised as the wisest of the original Milesian line, he ruled his kingdom from the Great Hall of Tara, aided by a loyal retinue of 1,150 people.

Through the Heremonian line of monarchs, the O'Sheas can also trace a descent from Corc, one of the sons of Cairbre Musc who, in turn, was a son of Conaire, the 111th Ard Rí of the Emerald Isle who died in about 165 A.D.

The Irish annals record how, during Cairbre Musc's reign as king of Munster, the province was blighted by a series of terrible misfortunes that included a catastrophic failure of the crops.

The reason for this, it was believed, was that Cairbre had grossly offended the Celtic deities by committing the sin of incest – fathering Corc through his sister Dubinn and also fathering another son, Cormac.

Hoping to appease the gods and alleviate the sufferings of Munster, the province's sub-kings demanded that Corc and Cormac, the fruits of Cairbre's illicit union with his sister, be burned by fire and their ashes scattered in a running stream.

This was carried out in the case of Cormac, but Dinach the Druid insisted that Corc be spared and placed under his protection.

What is now the barony of Iveragh in Co. Kerry became the territory of the O'Shea descendants of Corc, and it was here that they thrived up until the late twelfth century.

Ireland was far from being a unified nation in the late twelfth century, as rival chieftains battled with one another in attempts to gain dominance.

It was this disunity that opened the door to the Cambro-Norman invasion of the island, and the subsequent consolidation of the power of the English Crown.

This dominion over the island was ratified through the Treaty of Windsor of 1175, under the terms of which Irish chieftains were allowed to rule territory unoccupied by the Normans only in the role of vassals of the English monarch.

As further waves of ambitious and land-hungry Anglo-Norman adventurers descended on the island, the plight of the native Irish such as the O'Sheas became desperate.

One indication of the harsh treatment they had to endure can be found in a desperate plea sent to Pope John XII by Roderick O'Carroll of Ely, Donald O'Neill of Ulster, and a number of other Irish chieftains in 1318.

They stated: 'As it very constantly happens, whenever an Englishman, by perfidy or craft, kills an Irishman, however noble, or however innocent, be he clergy or layman, there is no penalty or correction enforced against the person who may be guilty of such wicked murder.

'But rather the more eminent the person killed and the higher rank which he holds among his own people, so much more is the murderer honoured and rewarded by the English, and not merely by the people at large, but also by the religious and bishops of the English race.'

This plea had no effect whatsoever on their treatment and, abandoning written appeals in favour of the sword, many took recourse in rebellion while others struggled to seek an accommodation with the power of the Crown while attempting to retain their ancient rights and privileges.

Chapter three:
The Ten Tribes

**The O'Sheas had not only to contend with the
encroachment on their lands of Anglo-Norman
adventurers, but also with the power of neighbouring
Gaelic-Irish clans.**

As the island became the scene of rapidly shifting
alliances and counter-alliances, the O'Sheas fell victim to
the power of the mighty McCarthys – who drove them off
their Co. Kerry lands.

The O'Sheas found a new home in Cloran, in Co.
Tipperary – and here they remained until the fifteenth
century when they relocated to Co. Kilkenny.

Bowing to English pressure, they prudently 'anglicised'
their proud Gaelic name to 'Shee' and 'Shethe' and soon
began to thrive as landowners and prominent civic officials.

Along with the families of Archer, Archdekin, Cowley,
Knaresborough, Langton, Lawless, Ley, Ragget and Rothes,
they became known as one of the Ten Tribes of Kilkenny.

Considered the most prominent of the 'ten tribes', the
O'Sheas produced a number of civic officials of the city of
Kilkenny – including Robert Shee who, in the closing years
of the fifteenth century, was known as the 'sovereign', or
chief burgess, of the city.

The O'Shea influence on Kilkenny can be seen in the

city to this day, not only in the form of the family tombs in the Church of St. Mary, but also in the form of what today is the Visitor Information Centre for Kilkenny in the city's Rose Inn Street.

Also known as Shee's Alm House, it was originally built in 1582 by Sir Richard Shee as the 'Hospital of Jesus at Kilkenny'.

While the O'Sheas, in the main, respectably flourished as law-abiding citizens, some of the name rebelled in dramatic form against the authorities in the mid-seventeenth century.

It was in 1641 that landowners rebelled against the English Crown's policy of settling, or 'planting' loyal Protestants on Irish land.

This policy had started during the reign from 1491 to 1547 of Henry VIII, whose Reformation effectively outlawed the established Roman Catholic faith throughout his dominions.

In the insurrection that exploded in 1641, at least 2,000 Protestant settlers were massacred while thousands more were stripped of their belongings and driven from their lands to seek refuge where they could.

England had its own distractions with the Civil War that culminated in the execution of Charles I in 1649, and from 1641 to 1649 Ireland was ruled by a rebel group known as the Irish Catholic Confederation, or the Confederation of Kilkenny.

The confederation held what is known as the National Assembly in Kilkenny in October of 1642, and there is a long-standing tradition that the venue for this was the residence of the Kilkenny civic official Robert Shee.

Shee, certainly, was among a number of people later accused of having induced the Governor of Kilkenny, Lord Mountjoy, into throwing in his lot with the rebels.

The rebellion was brutally and decisively crushed when England's 'Lord Protector', Oliver Cromwell, descended on the island at the head of a 20,000-strong army in August of 1649.

He had three main aims.

These were to quash all forms of rebellion, to 'remove' all Catholic landowners who had taken part in the rebellion, and to convert the native Irish to the Protestant faith – something that some O'Sheas, in common with other Catholics, had either prudently done previously or did so later.

Cromwell soon held the land in a grip of iron, allowing him to implement what amounted to a policy of ethnic cleansing.

An estimated 11 million acres of land were confiscated and the dispossessed native Irish banished to Connacht and Co. Clare, while an edict was issued stating that any native Irish found east of the River Shannon after May 1, 1654, faced either summary execution or transportation to the West Indies.

Among those O'Sheas whose lands were forfeited for their part in the rebellion were a Robert O'Shea and an Elias O'Shea.

One of the most famous bearers of the O'Shea name – although some of her detractors would prefer the description of 'infamous' – was Katharine O'Shea, also known as Katie O'Shea, but better known to posterity as Kitty O'Shea.

It was through her relationship with the Irish Protestant landowner and nationalist leader Charles Stewart Parnell that she became embroiled in one of the most notorious scandals of the late nineteenth century – one that led to the destruction of Parnell's political career.

Born Katharine Wood in 1846 in Braintree, Essex, she was of truly aristocratic English roots – with her father being Sir John Page Wood, 2nd Baronet of the name.

She was also a niece of Lord Hatherley, the Chancellor of the Exchequer in the Liberal Government of William Gladstone.

This was at a time when there was great pressure on the British Government to grant Home Rule to Ireland – and at the head of the Home Rule movement was Parnell, founder and leader of the Irish Parliamentary Party in the Parliament of Great Britain and Ireland.

Katharine first met the charismatic and fiery orator Parnell in 1880, by which time she was married to Captain William O'Shea, the Catholic Nationalist Member of Parliament for the borough of Galway.

She and Parnell embarked on their relationship shortly after their first meeting, with Parnell setting up home with her in a London suburb and later fathering three of her children.

Katharine and Captain O'Shea had by this time separated, but it was not until 1889 that he filed for divorce – one theory being that he had delayed divorce proceedings until then in the hope of inheriting money through his wife's extremely wealthy aunt.

But when the aunt died, leaving all her money to her cousins and not a penny to her niece Katharine, Captain O'Shea, with now nothing left to lose apart from what he considered his slighted honour, brought about divorce proceedings that cited Parnell as co-respondent.

The illicit love affair between Parnell and Katharine had been well known for some time among close-knit establishment circles, but when it became known to the wider public through the published details of the divorce proceedings, an outraged and vitriolic campaign rooted in so-called Victorian 'morality' was launched against the hapless pair.

The scandal led to Parnell's political fall in December of 1890 – his only consolation being that he was able to marry Katharine shortly after her divorce from Captain O'Shea was finalised.

By this time Katharine had been dubbed 'Kitty' by the scandal-raking newspapers of the time and his political enemies – who gleefully recognised that 'Kitty' was not only an abbreviated form of 'Katharine', but also a slang term for a prostitute.

Parnell, the broken man who had been the great shining hope of the cause of Irish nationalism, died only four short months after his marriage to the woman who had undoubtedly been the great love of his life.

Unfairly vilified by many for her role in Parnell's sad fall from grace and political influence, she died in 1921.

Chapter four:
On the world stage

Generations of bearers of the O'Shea name, in all its variety of spellings, have achieved fame and distinction through a wide range of pursuits, and not least in the world of acting.

Born in 1913 in Cardiff, **Tessie O'Shea** was the Welsh actress whose debut as an entertainer was on the stage of British music hall.

She was aged only six when she appeared on stage beside her cousin Adam Dionne in *The Wonder of Wales*, while by the time she was a teenager she had become popular as an actress in a number of BBC Radio broadcasts.

Appearing on stage in the 1930s, the young actress took advantage of her decidedly well-built proportions by adopting *Two Ton Tessie from Tennessee* as her theme song, while by the 1940s she was one of the stars of the London Palladium.

She also enjoyed success in the post-war years as a recording artist, while in 1963 she starred to great acclaim as the fish and chips peddler Ada Cockle in Noel Coward's Broadway musical *The Girl Who Came to Supper*.

This won her a Tony Award for Best Featured Actress in a Musical, while she appeared a year later on one of the most watched television shows in the history of American television.

This was on the Ed Sullivan Show, where she shared the bill with the Beatles – bringing her to even more popular attention.

Her role in the 1968 television movie *The Strange Case of Dr. Jekyll and Mr. Hyde* earned her an Emmy Award nomination for Outstanding Performance by an Actress in a Supporting Role in a Drama, while on the silver screen she appeared in films that included *London Town*, *The Blue Lamp* and, co-starring with Angela Lansbury, *Bedknobs and Broomsticks*.

The versatile and talented actress died in 1995.

In the original O'Shea homeland of Ireland, **Milo O'Shea** is the character actor who was born in 1926 in Dublin and who, after a career on stage, moved in the 1960s to an equally successful career in film.

His memorable film roles include that of Leopold Bloom in the 1967 screen version of James Joyce's *Ulysses*, the 1968 screen version of *Romeo and Juliet*, the 1968 *Barbarella*, the 1973 *Theatre of Blood* and, from 1982, *The Verdict*.

On television he achieved popularity in the BBC sitcom *Me Mammy*, co-starring with Yootha Joyce, while in more recent times he has had guest roles in the American political drama *The West Wing*.

Behind the camera lens, **John O'Shea** was the New Zealand independent filmmaker, director, producer and writer who was born in 1920 in New Plymouth and who died in 2001.

Responsible for the setting up in 1952, along with Roger Mirams, of Pacific Films, he was behind a number of New Zealand-based feature films that include the 1952 *Broken Barrier*, the 1964 *Runaway* and, from 1966, *Don't Let It Get You*.

Honoured with an O.B.E. in 1990 and a founder nine years earlier of the New Zealand Film Archive, he was also a recipient of the New Zealand Medal for services to the film industry.

In the highly competitive world of sport, William Alfred Shea, better known as **Bill Shea**, was the prominent lawyer, entrepreneur and baseball fan responsible for the return of National League Baseball to his home city of New York following the departure of the New York Giants and Brooklyn Dodgers after the 1957 season.

Born in 1907, Shea, who died in 1991, had his name immortalised in New York's Shea Stadium – the baseball venue named after him and which was the home ground of the New York Mets National League professional team from 1964 to 2008.

A multi-purpose stadium, it was also the home of the New York Jets until 1983, while in August of 1965 it was the venue for one of the biggest concerts in American pop music history.

This was the famous performance by the Beatles before

55,600 screaming fans at the opening of their 1965 North American tour.

At the time of writing, the stadium is being demolished to make way for a new development.

Also in baseball, **John Shea**, nicknamed 'Lefty', was the relief pitcher in Major League Baseball who was born in 1904 in Everett, Massachusetts, and who died in 1956.

Shea, who batted and threw left-handed, played for the Boston Red Sox during the 1928 season.

On the fields of European football, **Jay O'Shea** is the Republic of Ireland winger and striker who was born in 1988 and who, at the time of writing, plays for Galway United, while **John O'Shea**, born in 1981 in Waterford, is the Irish striker who, at the time of writing, plays for top English Premier League team Manchester United.

In American football, **Michael O'Shea** is the Canadian linebacker born in Toronto in 1970 and who, at the time of writing, plays for the Toronto Argonauts.

In the rough and tumble of the game of rugby, **John O'Shea**, born in 1940, is the former Welsh international rugby union player who, as a prop, was capped five times for his nation between 1967 and 1968.

Born in 1933 in Ayr, Queensland, **Kel O'Shea** is the former Australian rugby league player who is rated as having been among his nation's best players of the 20th century, having made 15 test and five World Cup appearances for this country.

Also on the rugby pitch, **Jerry Shea** was the Welsh international rugby union centre who was born in Newport in 1892.

Not only a rugby player, Shea, who died in 1947, was also an accomplished boxer and talented swimmer.

'O'Shea' is also found as a forename – commonly as a variant of 'Joshua' – and one of the most famous contemporary bearers of the name is O'Shea Jackson, born in 1969 in Los Angeles and better known as the rapper, record producer, actor, screenwriter, film director and producer **Ice Cube**.

He started to write rap while in High School, and continued while studying architectural drafting at the Phoenix Institute of Technology.

Turning his back on a career in architecture, he helped to develop what is known as 'gangsta rap' – and his often-controversial lyrics cover topics that include politics and ethnic discrimination.

His records include the 1990 *Kill at Will*, the 2006 *Laugh Now, Cry Later* and the 2008 *Raw Footage*, while films in which he has appeared include the 1991 *Boyz N the Hood* and the 2008 *First Sunday*.

He was also the director and executive producer of the 1995 *Friday* and writer and producer of the 2000 *Next Friday*.

In a decidedly different music genre, George Beverly Shea is the legendary singer and songwriter of gospel music more popularly known as **Bev Shea**.

Born in 1909 in Winchester, Ontario, he began singing in a church choir and, after he and his family moved to upstate New York, he found work in commercial radio.

Later moving to Chicago, he wrote and sang popular gospel music for religious broadcasts, and this led to an association over many years with the Billy Graham Evangelistic Association.

He was inducted in 1978 into the Gospel Music Hall of Fame in recognition of his lifelong contribution to gospel music.

In the world of political activism, **Alicia O'Shea Petersen** was the Tasmanian social reformer and suffragist who was born in 1862 and died in 1923.

Her cousin was John Earle, founder of the Workers' Political League and who in 1909 became Tasmania's first Labour Premier.

In 1913 she became the first woman in Tasmania to stand as a political candidate in a federal seat, while nine years later, when women were first allowed to stand for the Tasmanian House of Assembly, she stood for the Denison constituency.

Born in 1906, Clarence Lyell O'Shea, more popularly known as **Clarrie O'Shea,** was the Australian trades union activist whose imprisonment led to one of the biggest nationwide strikes in Australian labour history.

Secretary of the Victorian State section of the Australian Tramway and Motor Omnibus Employees' Association, he was jailed in 1969 for contempt of court when he disobeyed a court order for his union to pay $8,100 in fines under penal sections of the Conciliation and Arbitration Act.

A 'Free Clarrie and repeal the penal powers' campaign was mounted and led to an estimated one million workers throughout Australia downing tools for six days.

He was released from prison and the dispute ended when a man who claimed to have won the New South Wales lottery paid the fines.

O'Shea died in 1988.

In contemporary politics, **Brian O'Shea** is the Republic of Ireland Labour Party politician who was born in 1944 in Co. Waterford.

Elected to Dáil Éireann, the Irish Parliament, in 1989 as the member for Waterford, at the time of writing he is the party's spokesperson for Community, Rural and Gaeltacht Affairs.

In the world of academia, **John Gilmary Shea** was the American writer and historian who was born to Irish immigrant parents in New York City in 1824 and who died in 1892.

A noted historian of both American history and American Catholic history, he was also the first recipient of the University of Notre Dame's prestigious Laetare Medal.

In contemporary times, **Professor Sir Timothy O'Shea**, who was born in 1949 in Hamburg and raised in London, is the specialist in educational technology research who, at the time of writing, has been Vice-Chancellor and Principal of Edinburgh University, in Scotland, since 2002.

Elected a fellow of the Royal Society of Edinburgh in 2004 and knighted in 2008, he also at the time of writing sits on the boards of Scottish Enterprise, the Intermediary Technology Institute Scotland Ltd., and the British Council.

In the creative world of art, **O'Shea and Whelan** was a noted mid-nineteenth century Irish family concern of sculptors and stonemasons.

It was the brothers **James** and **John O'Shea** and their nephew Edward Whelan who literally stamped their mark on the buildings of Dublin, with their imaginative florid and gothic carvings.

One famous carving, to be seen to this day above a window on the city's Kildare Street Club, depicts the club members as monkeys playing billiards.

In contemporary times, one bearer of the O'Shea name involved in a particularly dangerous pursuit is **Mark O'Shea**, the herpetologist (reptile expert), photographer, author, lecturer and television personality who was born in 1956 in Wolverhampton, England.

Best known for his *O'Shea's Dangerous Reptiles* television show, he narrowly escaped in 1993 after being bitten by a Canebreak Rattlesnake while on one of his many reptilian excursions.

Key dates in Ireland's history from the first settlers to the formation of the Irish Republic:

circa 7000 B.C. Arrival and settlement of Stone Age people.

circa 3000 B.C. Arrival of settlers of New Stone Age period.

circa 600 B.C. First arrival of the Celts.

200 A.D. Establishment of Hill of Tara, Co. Meath, as seat of the High Kings.

circa 432 A.D. Christian mission of St. Patrick.

800-920 A.D. Invasion and subsequent settlement of Vikings.

1002 A.D. Brian Boru recognised as High King.

1014 Brian Boru killed at battle of Clontarf.

1169-1170 Cambro-Norman invasion of the island.

1171 Henry II claims Ireland for the English Crown.

1366 Statutes of Kilkenny ban marriage between native Irish and English.

1529-1536 England's Henry VIII embarks on religious Reformation.

1536 Earl of Kildare rebels against the Crown.

1541 Henry VIII declared King of Ireland.

1558 Accession to English throne of Elizabeth I.

1565 Battle of Affane.

1569-1573 First Desmond Rebellion.

1579-1583 Second Desmond Rebellion.

1594-1603 Nine Years War.

1606 Plantation' of Scottish and English settlers.

1607	Flight of the Earls.
1632-1636	Annals of the Four Masters compiled.
1641	Rebellion over policy of plantation and other grievances.
1649	Beginning of Cromwellian conquest.
1688	Flight into exile in France of Catholic Stuart monarch James II as Protestant Prince William of Orange invited to take throne of England along with his wife, Mary.
1689	William and Mary enthroned as joint monarchs; siege of Derry.
1690	Jacobite forces of James defeated by William at battle of the Boyne (July) and Dublin taken.
1691	Athlone taken by William; Jacobite defeats follow at Aughrim, Galway, and Limerick; conflict ends with Treaty of Limerick (October) and Irish officers allowed to leave for France.
1695	Penal laws introduced to restrict rights of Catholics; banishment of Catholic clergy.
1704	Laws introduced constricting rights of Catholics in landholding and public office.
1728	Franchise removed from Catholics.
1791	Foundation of United Irishmen republican movement.
1796	French invasion force lands in Bantry Bay.
1798	Defeat of Rising in Wexford and death of United Irishmen leaders Wolfe Tone and Lord Edward Fitzgerald.